URANUS

by Emma Bassier

Cody Koala
An Imprint of Pop!
popbooksonline.com

abdobooks.com
Published by Pop!, a division of ABDO, PO Box 398166, Minneapolis, Minnesota 55349. Copyright © 2021 by POP, LLC. International copyrights reserved in all countries. No part of this book may be reproduced in any form without written permission from the publisher. Pop!™ is a trademark and logo of POP, LLC.

Printed in the United States of America, North Mankato, Minnesota.

102020
012021

THIS BOOK CONTAINS RECYCLED MATERIALS

Cover Photo: Mark Garlick/Science Source
Interior Photos: Mark Garlick/Science Source, 1, 13, 20–21; iStockphoto, 5, 17; Mark Garlick/Science Photo Library/Alamy, 6; Roger Harris/Science Source, 9 (top); Shutterstock Images, 9 (bottom left), 10, 14 (Uranus), 14 (Sun), 19 (top); NASA, 9 (bottom right), 19 (bottom left); Walter Myers/Science Source, 19 (bottom right)

Editor: Alyssa Krekelberg
Series Designer: Colleen McLaren

Library of Congress Control Number: 2020940267
Publisher's Cataloging-in-Publication Data
Names: Bassier, Emma, author.
Title: Uranus / by Emma Bassier
Description: Minneapolis, Minnesota : POP!, 2021 | Series: Planets | Includes online resources and index
Identifiers: ISBN 9781532169137 (lib. bdg.) | ISBN 9781532169496 (ebook)
Subjects: LCSH: Uranus (Planet)--Juvenile literature. | Planets--Juvenile literature. | Solar system--Juvenile literature. | Milky Way--Juvenile literature. | Space--Juvenile literature.
Classification: DDC 523.47--dc23

Hello! My name is

Cody Koala

Pop open this book and you'll find QR codes like this one, loaded with information, so you can learn even more!

Scan this code* and others like it while you read, or visit the website below to make this book pop.

popbooksonline.com/uranus

*Scanning QR codes requires a web-enabled smart device with a QR code reader app and a camera.

Table of Contents

Chapter 1
The Seventh Planet 4

Chapter 2
An Ice Giant 8

Chapter 3
Spinning Sideways. 12

Chapter 4
Moons and Rings 18

Making Connections 22
Glossary. 23
Index 24
Online Resources 24

Chapter 1

The Seventh Planet

Eight planets **orbit** the Sun. The Sun is the star at the center of our **solar system**. Uranus is the seventh planet from the Sun.

Watch a video here!

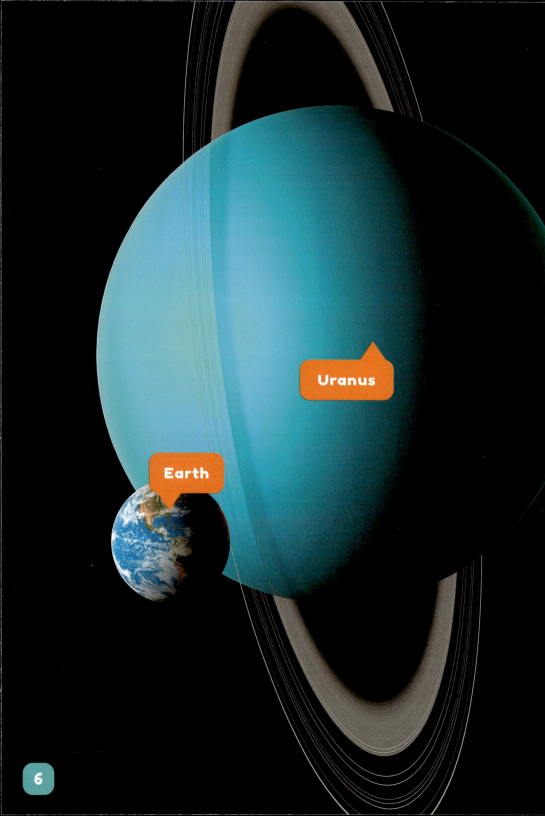

Uranus is the third-largest planet. It is approximately four times wider than Earth.

> Uranus is named after the Greek god of the sky.

Chapter 2

An Ice Giant

Uranus is far from the Sun. It gets little heat and light. It is windy and cold. Uranus is a blue-green color. This color comes from methane gas in its **atmosphere**.

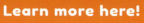

What makes up Uranus?

atmosphere made of gases

mantle made of icy materials

core made of rock

Uranus is an ice giant. It is large and mostly made up of gases and icy materials. The planet does not have a hard surface to stand on. Deep inside the planet is a small, rocky core.

Chapter 3

Spinning Sideways

Uranus **orbits** the Sun. One lap around the Sun is one year. A year on Uranus lasts approximately 84 Earth years.

Learn more here!

Uranus

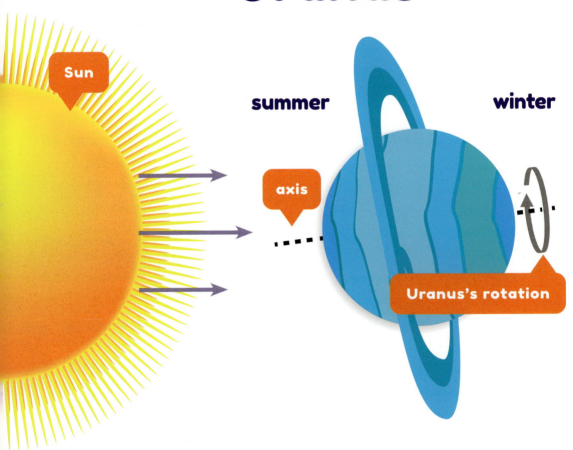

Uranus spins on its **axis**. One complete spin is one day. A day on Uranus lasts 17 hours. Uranus does not spin at a slight tilt like some other planets. Its axis is very tilted. Uranus spins on its side.

> Scientists think something very large hit Uranus long ago and caused the planet's tilt.

Because of this extreme tilt, Uranus has very long seasons. Each season lasts 21 Earth years. But the planet's tilt means one side of Uranus sees the Sun for 42 years. During this time, the other side is cold and dark.

> Seasons on Earth last between 90 to 93 days.

Chapter 4

Moons and Rings

Scientists have found 27 moons around Uranus. But there could be even more. The moons are named after characters from famous plays and stories.

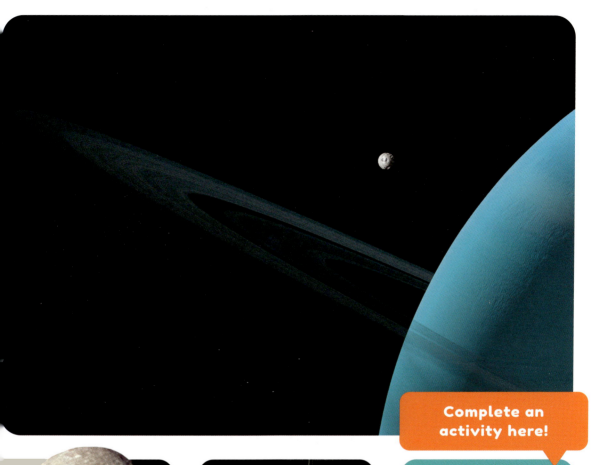

Complete an activity here!

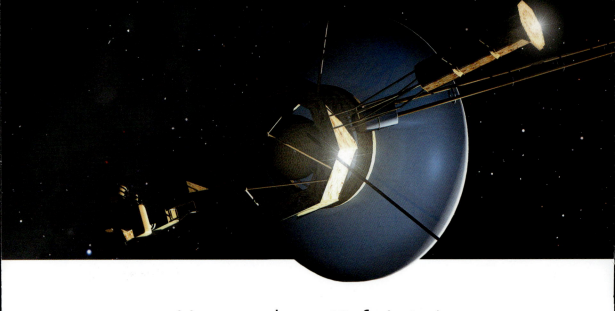

Uranus has 13 faint rings. They are made of dust and chunks of rock. Some rings are thin and gray.

Uranus also has one blue ring and one red ring.

The *Voyager 2* is the only **spacecraft** that has flown by Uranus to study it.

Making Connections

Text-to-Self

Would you want to travel to space? Why or why not?

Text-to-Text

Have you read other books about planets? How are those planets similar to or different from Uranus?

Text-to-World

Uranus and Earth are both planets. What do they have in common? What makes Uranus unique?

Glossary

atmosphere – the layers of gases that surround a planet.

axis – an imaginary line that runs through the middle of a planet.

orbit – to follow a rounded path around another object.

solar system – a collection of planets and other space material orbiting a star.

spacecraft – a vehicle that is used to explore space.

Index

axis, 14, 15

ice giant, 11

moons, 18

orbit, 4, 12

rings, 20–21

seasons, 14, 16

solar system, 4

Sun, 4, 8, 12, 14, 16

Online Resources

popbooksonline.com

Thanks for reading this Cody Koala book!

Scan this code* and others like it in this book, or visit the website below to make this book pop!

popbooksonline.com/uranus

*Scanning QR codes requires a web-enabled smart device with a QR code reader app and a camera.